THE WORLD

After Czeslaw Milosz

THE WORLD

After Czeslaw Milosz

poems by

MRB Chelko

Dream Horse Press
California

Dream Horse Press
www.dreamhorsepress.com
Editor: J.P. Dancing Bear

Dream Horse Press
Post Office Box 2080
Aptos, California 95001-2080
U.S.A.

Chelko, MRB
      The World
            p.40

              ISBN 978-1-935716-14-3
              1. Poetry

10 9 8 7 6 5 4 3 2 1

First Edition

Cover: "Break" by Rain Jordan
http://rainjordanart.com

Contents

THE WORLD

After Czeslaw Milosz

Nicholas John

The Road

We were ourselves, even then, somehow. Armed
with trusty pencil-case. Bright pictures
real and stuffed in our backpacks. The other kids

got scared maybe as we skipped along. The road
stretched inside us and out. Your hair
grew in branches. We had mountains on our shoulders,

beautiful ones. Was it then the things, like cancer and
flower beds, mixed beneath our T-shirts? You know, I still
search those roadside weeds for the sharpened crayons we lost.

The Gate

Wild pigeons have covered its lantern completely, but it held
once, the light of a summer evening. Its blue glow, an eye

opened under water. Something you have to keep seeing. Now, dogs
and loaves of bread block the gate. Eat both. Coo until it's not a gate;

it's a harp strung with your hair. Play a distant song, or a song, at least,
of distance. The touch of your hands can polish even this.

The Porch

knelt beneath our scenes of battle,
both of us: dark vials glinting
as the sun warmed our backdoor.
We played helpless
children launching great
warships across a plastic table—
ourselves, a small-toed kind
of fear.

But my eyes are pink tongues at night.
Oh yeah? *I can use this piece of bark to make the world
disappear completely.*

Who cares? I can steal your breath and hold it in.
If you steal my breath, I'll stretch your lungs over the linden tree.

The Dining Room

You said a crowd of people mingling
in a room with low windows best depicts
winter. But
I remember how mother prayed alone

for snow in the corner. Her belly no longer big enough
for us to roll inside, be warm. *Don't sit
on the reupholstered chairs! Little devils
will eat you!* I still believe the smoke

from our chimney
threatened neighborhood trees. That our
clocks housed the darkest birds.

The Stairs

The curved steps narrowed as mother
dragged down her enormous shadow.
My foot, a boar's head, struggled
at the base of the steps. I knew
with the first step I would smash
the face of the boar. Mother
sniffed. The curved steps
flickered. If I was careful, the boar
could live, and the steps could
smell of wax, not her robe
tied at the waist, not
her tall walk
slowly.

Pictures

In the photo book I found mostly people
I didn't recognize. So, I looked instead

for grandfather's exploded fingers
in the crudely trimmed image of a European city.

No luck. But, a very dead moth fell
into my lap as I turned the page.

Father in the Library

God often falls out the window, so father
reads with a high forehead—or
God's forehead is so high, father falls from his bookshelf
trying to reach it...   I can read, but
instead I lick the dust from father's books. They smell
so good I have to know.

Father's Incantations

You are great. Small, but great.
Whether you were once perfect,
no one remembers.

From the Window

We can look like a family of tulips
but, at night, we roll on the floor,
wrapped in the silver thread

of each others' dreams. When we wake up
the house is a like a boat inside
a house. We eat breakfast. Father says

finally, he can see clearly. And Mother tells
the goose feather floating in her cereal
Americans eat like this all the time.

Father Explains

Once, only rain divided land from the white
foam clouds; its bluish mist roamed the dark

forests alone. One day, a herd of bridges charged down
from the sky to keep the rain company. They brought castles

and fine cities until the rain could reach only pretty glass
roofs. So, the rain died, but stayed famous.

A Parable of the Poppy

Even though she'd buried
all the planets and stars
in her garden, the girl
did not feel better.

So, she planted poppies
to brighten up her little house.
At dusk, when she finished planting,
a dog barked softly.

That night, she was crushed in her bed
by more poppies than you can
imagine—some with roots bigger
than the earth.

By the Peonies

For one short instant, a long time ago, my mother
became a swarm of tiny beetles—
1,000 gleaming black faces, she swayed
the green leaves. Now

she stands by the peony bed. The peonies
in bloom, white and pink, lap at her ankles.
If she reaches for even one, she'll let go
the children and herself and speckles of light
she thinks.

Faith

I close my eyes
whenever I see
you know
a sharp rock
a dew drop
because they have
been around
always
like hurt
or the leaf floating
in me
grow flowers
rocks
strength to live
on the earth
with (close your eyes)
the long shadows I must
cast down
to dream things
(trees full)
up

Hope

Imagine, all the living
flesh you have ever seen: a garden
discovered on an unnamed star.
We cannot turn away
from the world, what with
human touch still so
new in our beds.

And you.

All things seem more clearly
if you hope wisely.

Love

It doesn't matter
how my finger longs
to touch bruised fruit
(the near unpalatable
sweetness of those
tossed or dropped pieces, not
meant to be eaten,
darkening
among the many unpicked things),
because I have learned

without even knowing it

that the dark twitch of your lips,
the struggling animal of your lips,
always serves best
the heals of my heart.

The Excursion to the Forest

In my parents' home, the sun forfeits its flame
to a candlestick. They wander toward it; gold
light flows in their eyes.

But you and I lie still
young on the forest path, our long hair tangled
with the grass. When, finally, no sun lights the treetops,

we call, *Come back!* But hardly a whisper comes out.
We are tiny people—even close up. Lying here,
we must resemble flowers, picked, then dropped.

The Bird Kingdom

Bright, beautiful, warm, and free, your body
as if from the bottom of a lake, rises and floats, a golden lure
glinting on the surface of my mind, among feathers.

Fear

silent the night as a stone dying sucks away
its own meaning no end no terrible battle in the dark
                                    no fire
the forest is wild yes and something comes nearer
the hot breath no one speaks of I feel on my neck
the hand of a lost child
or father they will die forever kids the night
has no end the bushes sway what's behind them
will save us or swallow us whole

Recovery

is for lost things and broken people.
But we've arrived, Love. Let us rest at the edge

of the earth. As promised, it's still dark.

Heaven forbid the sun rise
now, dragging its bell.

Acknowledgments

Thank you to the editors of the following journals where some of these poems first appeared: *AGNI Online, Court Green, DIAGRAM, Forklift, Ohio, The National Poetry Review, Sun's Skeleton,* and *Washington Square Review.*

Thank you also to David Rivard, Charles Simic, Ann Joslin Williams, Sarah Stickney, Patrick Weatherly, Jenny Lynn Keller, Brian Wilkins, Michael Vizsolyi and Dan Rosenberg for their friendship, support, and help with this manuscript.

About the Author

MRB Chelko is a recent graduate of The University of New Hampshire's MFA program and Assistant Editor of the unbound journal, *Tuesday; An Art Project*. Her poems have appeared widely in journals and have been featured on *Verse Daily*. *What to Tell the Sleeping Babies*, her first chapbook, is available from sunnyoutside press

Previous winners of the Dream Horse Press National Poetry Chapbook Prize:

2009—*The Book of Evil* by Jason Bredle
2008—*Thirteen Curses (and other love poems)* by T.J. Beitlemen
2007—*Incorporated* by Charles Sweetman
2006—*The Small Anything City*, by Cynthia Arrieu-King
2005—*A Unified Theory of Light*, by Theodore Worozbyt
2004—*Wait for Me, I'm Gone*, by Amy Holman
2003—*Adam & Eve Go to the Zoo*, by Jason Gray
2002—*New Fables, Old Songs*, by Rob Carney
2001—*The Florida Letters*, by Ryan G. Van Cleave

www.ingramcontent.com/pod-product-compliance
Lightning Source LLC
Chambersburg PA
CBHW022348040426

42449CB00006B/777